MW01047903

Cover design and photographs by
Aaron Hirsh. www.aerox.net

Copyright © 2010 www.aquaexplorers.com
ISBN# 1450596150
EAN-13 9781450596152

Capt. Dan Berg is a P.A.D.I (Professional Association of Diving Instructors) Master Scuba Diver Trainer. He is a Specialty Instructor in Wreck Diving, Night Diving, Search and Recovery, Underwater Hunting, Deep Diving, Dry Suit Diving, U/W Metal Detecting, U/W Archeology, and has written his own nationally approved specialties in Shipwreck Research and U/W Cinematography. Capt. Berg owns and operates the 40' custom built Young Brothers charter boat Wreck Valley and is a member of the Eastern Dive Boat Association. Mr. Berg has authored over a dozen shipwreck and diving related books and was the host and producer of the award winning Dive Wreck Valley TV series. Capt. Dan received the prestigious BTS Diver of the Year Award in 1994. He also was a first year recipient of the SSI Platinum Pro 5000 Award. Mr. Berg holds 6 current US Patents for Diving Equipment design. Dan's photographs ,video and shipwreck articles have appeared on Fox 5 News, CNN, CBS, Skin Diver Magazine, plus many more.

Back in the early 1980's the author noticed a ship in a bottle on the shelf of one of his friends. When he inquired as to how it was made all he was told was that "it was not easy". The author went to the library, read a couple model building books, then sat down and built his first ship in a bottle. He makes no claims at being a master model maker. He is only someone that loves the ocean, maritime history and the art of crafting these miniature tall ships. Check out Capt. Berg's other PDF shipwreck and diving books:

http://www.aquaexplorers.com/e_books_downloadable.htm

Three masted fully rigged ship in a bottle. Crafted by Capt. Daniel Berg. Note the realistic water, lighthouse and island.

Table of Contents

Tall ship image courtesy Allposters.com

Building a Ship in a Bottle Model

About this book

Unlike other books on the subject, that provide a diagram and step by step instructions Capt. Dan attempts to teach model builders to understand the basic principals involved. After reading this heavily illustrated text, readers should have a good understanding of how to design rig and build both square sailed as well as fore and aft rigged vessels. They will then be able to apply the basic principles and techniques and build any type of sailing ship they choose. Please note that there are many different techniques used by different builders in creating their ship models. Some use elaborate mast hinges while others contend with a maze of rigging lines which all run through and under the hull. This book teaches Capt. Dan's basic and straight forward, simple techniques that he uses on all of his ship in a bottle models. These basics can be enhanced and modified as model builders become more proficient. Capt. Dan has included a showcase of ship in bottle images from some

Before beginning any model project check out as many ship designs as possible. Pay attention to the way these ships list to one side and to the sea conditions. Image courtesy Allposters.com.

of the best master model builders in the world. Often, the best way to improve ones skills and technique is to examine the exquisite work and detail of these masters.

History

The art of building a ship in a bottle dates back to the early 1800's. Sailors for centuries have crafted items during thier long journeys away from home. They worked with supplies that were readily available to them and are responsible for some of the finest scrimshaw and models ever created. Exactly when the first ship was built and inserted into a bottle is unknown. Bottles older than the mid 1800's were often not clear enough to showcase a miniature tall ship. By the late 1800's, good quality hand blown glass bottles were abundant. It was during this time that this craft was perfected. Models back then were often created out of whale bone and exotic hardwood. Many of these early examples are now housed in museums around the world. Unfortunately, times have changed for mariners and model builders. Far fewer of our youth now venture out to sea for adventure or to seek their fortune. With

Ship in a bottle models are built outside the bottle and designed to have it's masts and sails fold flat. Image courtesy Allposters.com

the advent of the internet and video games even fewer are spending any time carving or crafting any type of models. The goal of this book is to help stir up some interest in this ancient maritime art form and preserve the building techniques for future generations.

The Secret

Many people think that the miniature ship model is actually built piece by piece while inside the bottle. Others think it's a complete illusion and that the bottle is cut in half and then glued back together around the miniature model. Actually, the detailed ship model is built outside the bottle but it's designed in a way that allows it's masts and sails to fold flat. The model is then slid in through the bottles neck and then the masts are carefully pulled upright with string and a few handcrafted tools. Of course, it sounds a bit easier than it actually is. With the information and techniques provided in this text anyone with a little creativity will be able to craft and display a quality piece of maritime art.

Two masted schooner in a square bottle with glass stopper. Built by Daniel Berg/ Aaron Hirsh collection.

Materials
Appropriate bottle
Wood
Wood dowels (for masts)
Sand paper
Thread (black, tan)
Elmers Glue
Paper
Wire
Art tape
Oil based paint (for hull and details)
Blue oil based paint (for water)
Epoxy casting resin
Blue paint (for water)
Clear silicon
White silicone

A variation of a ship in a bottle is a ship in a lightbulb or globe. The trick is to use saran wrap to protect the glass from the putty. Once the ship is built and in place the water is lifted the saran wrap removed and the glass turned so that the putty seals the containers opening. Spanish Galleon built by Capt. Dan Berg.

Image courtesy Allposters.com

Tools
Needle nose pliers
Tweezers
Wire snips
Screw driver
Razor blade or razor knife
Needle &pins
Saw
Sand paper
Drill bits
Hand held dill (pin vise)
Wire coat hangers to make into tools

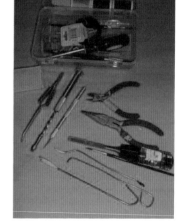

Additional (Optional) tools
Dremmel grinder
Pin saw

These twin racing schooners in a bottle were built by the author. The bottle is a late 1800's vintage one gallon water jug recovered while diving off Long Island NY's coast. Photo by Dan Berg.

Choosing the perfect Bottle

Picking an appropriate bottle is actually the first step in any ship in a bottle project. Your bottle should be clear, have a shape that will enhance and showcase the ship inside and should have a large diameter neck. Although it's not mandatory a cork style bottle is often preferred over modern screw tops. Keep in mind that square or triangular shaped bottles will sit independently on a display shelf. Round bottles will require a display mounting base to prevent them from rolling off the shelf. The choice of the exact bottle size and shape is entirely personal. New bottles are much clearer than antique glass but the old hand blown bottles of the late 1800's offer their own unique character. I actually prefer to use antique bottles. These bottles have nice cork stoppers but you have to be careful as many have small necks which may not be suitable for ships in bottles. As a scuba diver for over thirty years, I'm fortunate to be able to find a good assortment of old bottles while scuba diving in old harbors. My thought is that these antique glass bottles with their inherent imperfections add more character to the

Close up detail from previous page. Photo by Daniel

finished project. Fortunately, you do not have to be a scuba diver to find great old bottles. Any antique store should be able to provide you with a wide assortment to choose from. Pick a bottle with a large diameter, short neck and clear glass.

Once a bottle is chosen make sure it is clean and then completely dry. For new bottles this can be accomplished with soap and water. For antique or very dirty bottles this is the method we use for cleaning our bottles recovered while diving.

Cleaning Glass
Fortunately, glass holds up fairly well underwater, even after decades of submersion. Usually, bottles dating from the late 1800's to the present, found on or near shipwrecks, are in good condition. There are, of course, exceptions to every rule, and I have read reports of glass dating to the early 1700's that would crack after drying out. When intact bottles are found buried in silt or sand, they can be as clear as the day they were lost. However, if the

This wall mounted ship in a bottle was built by the author. Note the driftwood mount.

wreck is in a strong current area or in a location where a lot of surge is present, the bottles can be dulled by the sand blasting effect of constantly tumbling around. A sandblasted bottle like this is not suitable to be used for a ship in a bottle project.

In order to clean glass, all that is needed is fresh water, some powdered dish washing detergent and a little elbow grease. If stubborn stains are present, a 50% solution of muriatic acid and water can be used. Remember to wear plastic gloves and to rinse the artifact with fresh water after using acid. For bottles that are stained on the inside, use a bottle brush with a mud-like solution of dry dishwasher detergent and water. If you don't have a bottle brush, just shake the sloppy mixture around. It will have enough abrasiveness to remove most stains without damaging the glass. When finished, rinse with fresh water and let the bottle completely dry for several days.

For those that would rather have the benefit of modern crystal

Image courtesy Allposters.com

clear glass while still having a cork style neck a modern apothecary bottle may be the perfect choice. They are available in a variety of stores as well as on the internet. Best of all they only cost a few dollars each.

Types of sailing ships.
Picking the type of vessel for each project is a combination of what type of ship would look and fit best in the bottle you have chosen, your experience level and your own interest and creativity. Since I have been a shipwreck diver for over 3 decades I often create replicas of some of the shipwrecked vessels I have explored. Others pick certain types of vessels based entirely on appearance. The choice is yours. Keep in mind that the rigging on a vessel like a schooner with fore and aft rigged sails is much less complex and therefore easier to build than a square sailed ship. This book will provide details of how to rig both but you may want to build a fore and aft rigged schooner as your first ship in a bottle. Although there are many different types of sailing ships, I have listed some

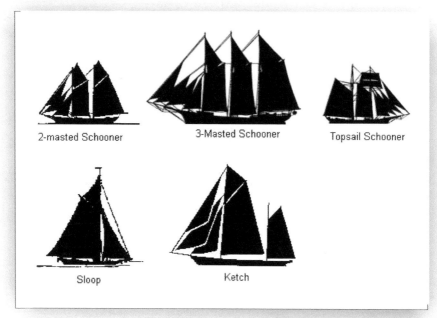

2-masted Schooner   3-Masted Schooner   Topsail Schooner

Sloop   Ketch

of the more popular for model builders. Please note that ship in a bottle builders are only limited by there own creativity. Any type of ship from tugboats to passenger liners can be built in a bottle. Please use the list below only as a small sample.

Barque
A sailing vessel with three or more masts. This type of craft has fore and aft rigged sails on her aftermast and is square rigged on all other masts.

Barkentine
This is a three-masted sailing ship that is square rigged on her fore mast only.

Brig
A two-masted sailing vessel. Both masts are square rigged. On the vessels stern mast she also has a gaff sail

Brigantine
This is a two-masted sailing vessel with her foremast being square rigged.

Full-rigged Ship

Brig

Brigantine

Hermaphrodite Brig

Bark or Barque

Barquentine

Cutter
Sailing vessel with one-mast rigged with a mainsail and two headsails.

Ketch
Two-masted sailboat with after mast being shorter. This type of vessels aftermast is foreward of her rudder post.

Knockabout
Sailing vessel very similar to a schooner but without a bowsprit.

Schooner
Sailing vessel with a least two masts and the mainmast being taller.

Topsail Schooner
A schooner with a square rigged sail on her forward mast.

Windjammer
Large square rigged sailing ship.

Hull Construction
Some model builders go as far as researching builders prints for each vessel and then converting them to scale. Others, like myself, use a little artistic license and just sketch a vessel that artistically fits the bottle chosen. I usually take a good look at the bottle of choice and figure out how long I want the hull to be. Also take into consideration how tall the masts can be and how the finished ship

Basic Principles

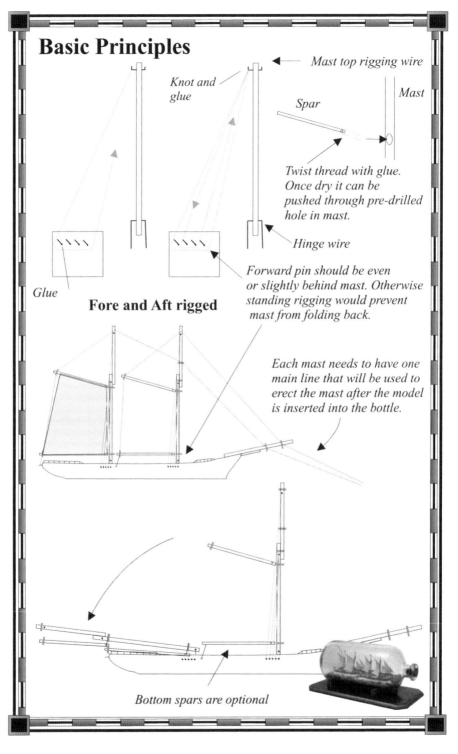

Mast top rigging wire

Knot and glue

Spar

Mast

Twist thread with glue. Once dry it can be pushed through pre-drilled hole in mast.

Hinge wire

Glue

Forward pin should be even or slightly behind mast. Otherwise standing rigging would prevent mast from folding back.

Fore and Aft rigged

Each mast needs to have one main line that will be used to erect the mast after the model is inserted into the bottle.

Bottom spars are optional

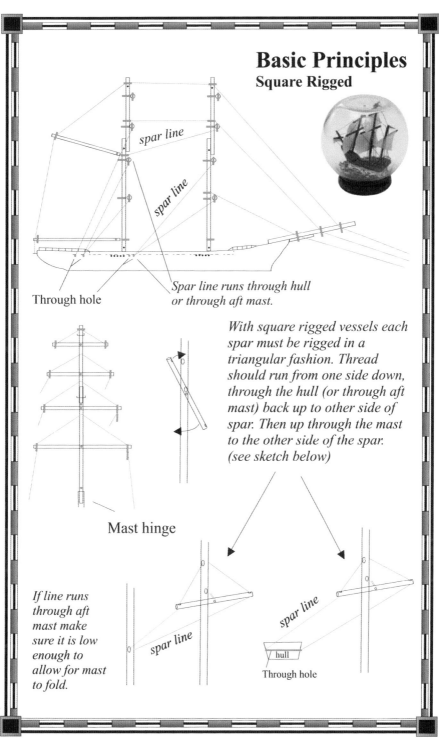

Basic Principles
Square Rigged

spar line

spar line

Spar line runs through hull or through aft mast.

Through hole

With square rigged vessels each spar must be rigged in a triangular fashion. Thread should run from one side down, through the hull (or through aft mast) back up to other side of spar. Then up through the mast to the other side of the spar. (see sketch below)

Mast hinge

If line runs through aft mast make sure it is low enough to allow for mast to fold.

spar line

spar line

hull

Through hole

Fully rigged ship in a bottle. Built by Capt. Dan Berg.

will look inside the bottle. It's highly recommended to draw a rough side view sketch of the ship with masts in place. When creating these sketches make sure that the total height of the hull is no larger than ½ the diameter of the bottles neck. If your bottle has a short neck you may be able to slightly increase this size. Basically, the hull with the additional height of the folded mast, rigging and sails have to be able to fit through the bottles opening. Refer to illustrations for details. You can then create a matching top view of the basic hull. I have included three sample sketches in this text. The first is for a fore and aft rigged vessel. The second is a two-masted square rigged ship, and the third is a three-masted square rigged ship. To use one of these sketch sets just scale it up or down with a copy machine until its size fits your bottle. Note that my sketch sets include all masts, spars sails and rigging. By printing the pages you can refer to each as you build each part of the model. You should also note that my rigging is designed to be taught when the masts are upright yet still be able to fold. This is done with only a few lines (one per mast) running through the ships bowsprit and out the bottles neck during construction.

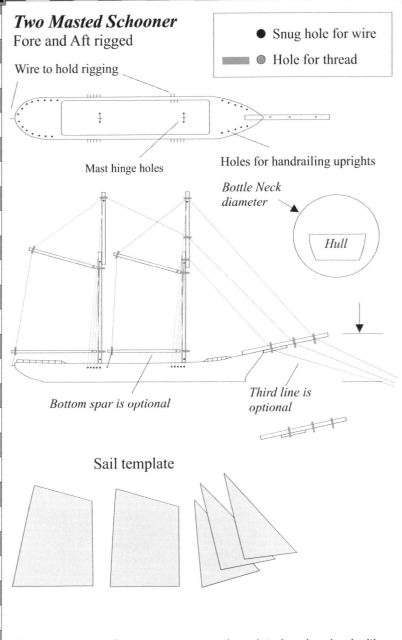

Two Masted Schooner
Fore and Aft rigged

●	Snug hole for wire
▬ ●	Hole for thread

Wire to hold rigging

Mast hinge holes

Holes for handrailing uprights

Bottle Neck diameter

Hull

Bottom spar is optional

Third line is optional

Sail template

This two-masted Schooner page can be printed and resized with copy machine so that the ship model fits the bottle of your choice. Sketch by Capt. Dan Berg.

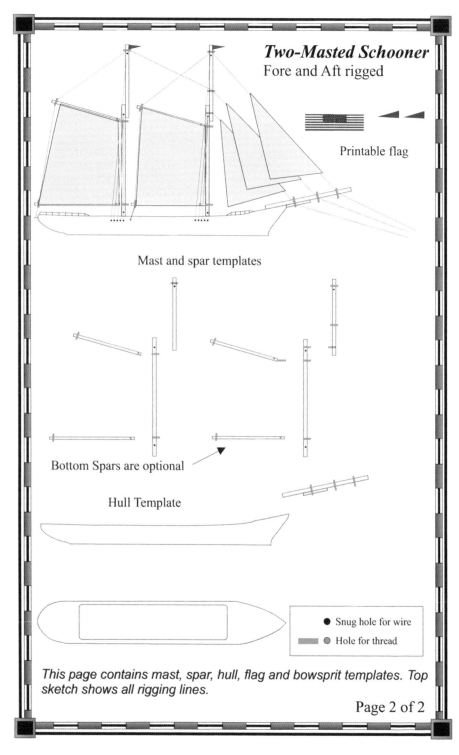

Two-Masted Schooner
Fore and Aft rigged

Printable flag

Mast and spar templates

Bottom Spars are optional

Hull Template

● Snug hole for wire

● Hole for thread

This page contains mast, spar, hull, flag and bowsprit templates. Top sketch shows all rigging lines.

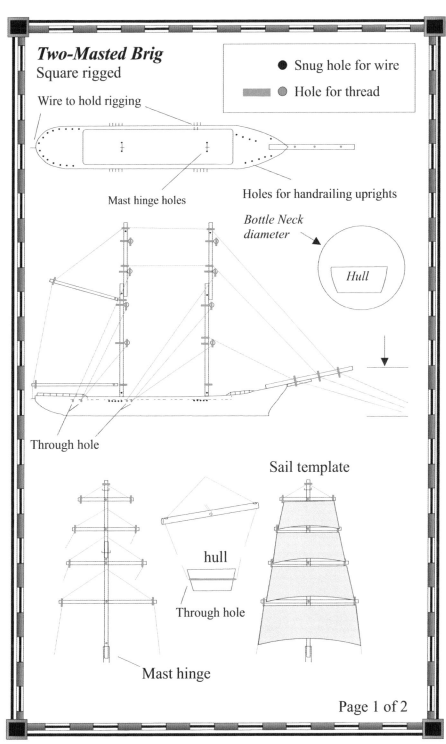

Two-Masted Brig
Square rigged

● Snug hole for wire
▬ ● Hole for thread

Wire to hold rigging

Mast hinge holes

Holes for handrailing uprights

Bottle Neck diameter

Hull

Through hole

Sail template

hull

Through hole

Mast hinge

Page 1 of 2

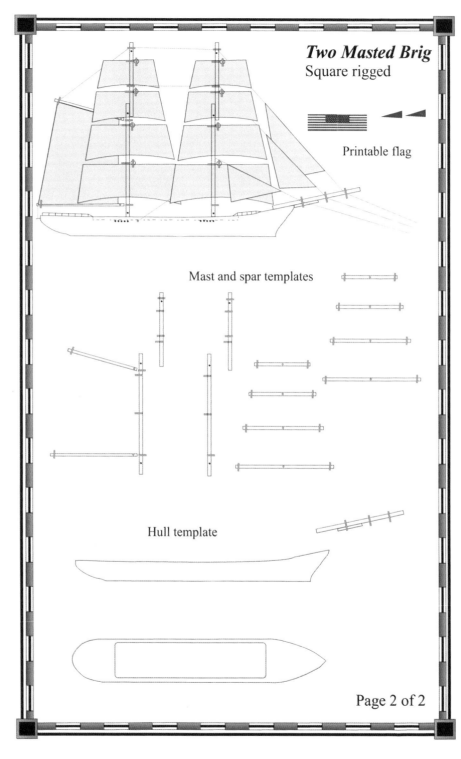

Two Masted Brig
Square rigged

Printable flag

Mast and spar templates

Hull template

Three-Masted Fully Rigged

- ● Snug hole for wire
- ▬▬ ● Hole for thread

Wire to hold rigging

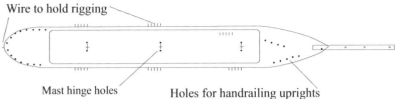

Mast hinge holes

Holes for handrailing uprights

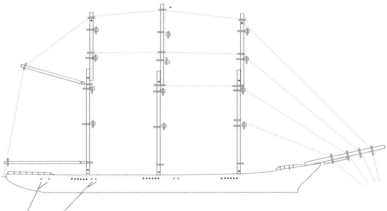

Through holes

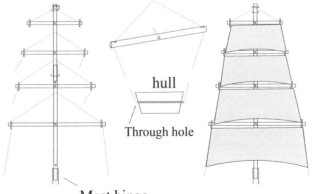

hull

Through hole

Mast hinge

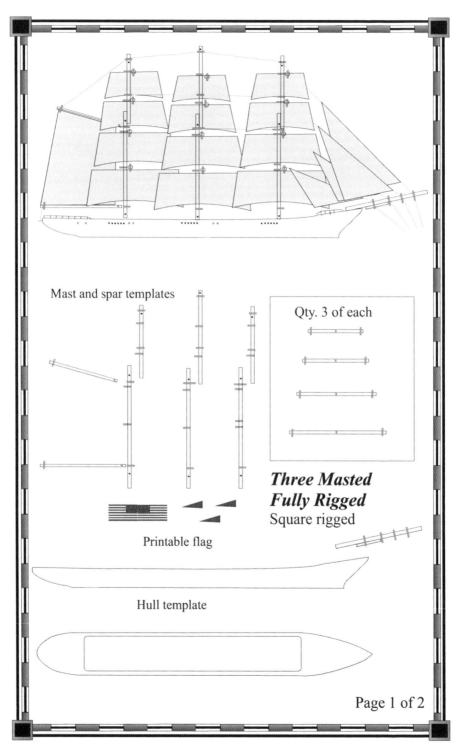

Mast and spar templates

Qty. 3 of each

**Three Masted
Fully Rigged**
Square rigged

Printable flag

Hull template

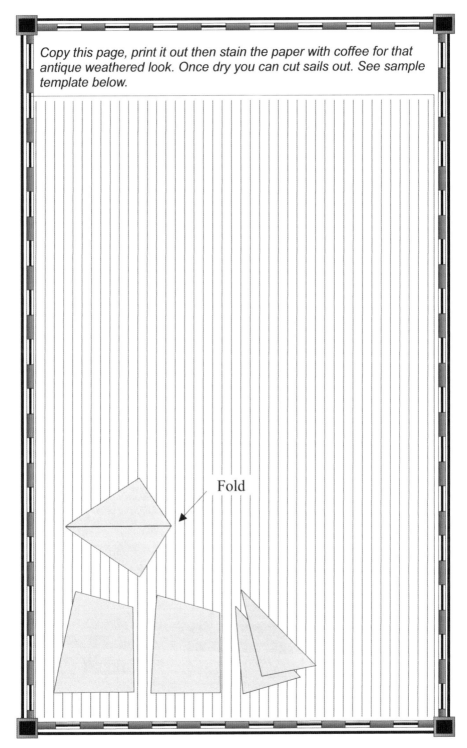

Copy this page, print it out then stain the paper with coffee for that antique weathered look. Once dry you can cut sails out. See sample template below.

Fold

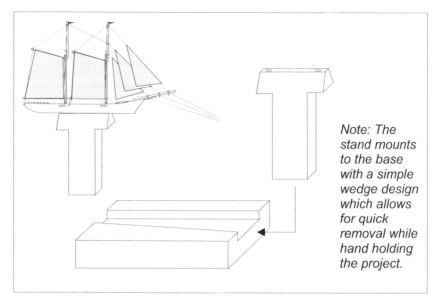

Note: The stand mounts to the base with a simple wedge design which allows for quick removal while hand holding the project.

Before even getting started with the ship's hull you will need to build a working stand for the model. The ship's hull will be screwed firmly in place to the mount which is removable from it's base. The stand makes it easy to hold onto the tiny model while working on the hull, rigging and details.

Screws secure hull to stand

One of the author's work stands with the start of a new project firmly held in place by two screws. Note: the stand is mounted to the base with a simple wedge design which allows for quick removal while hand holding the project.

Start by cutting out both the top and side view templates. These can be traced onto a piece of wood. You can use hardwood but it's much easier to work with pine. You can use a variety of tools to cut out and shape the hull. Some carve the entire hull by hand while others use a pin saw or band saw to make the rough cuts and a dremel sander to finish up the rough design.

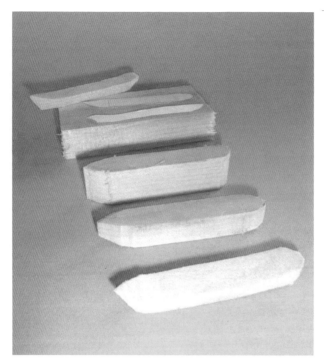

You can use a variety of tools to cut out and shape the hull.

Start by cutting out both the top and side view of the hull which are used as templates. These can be traced onto a piece of wood. You can use hardwood but it's much easier to work with pine. You can use a variety of tools to cut out and shape the hull. Some carve

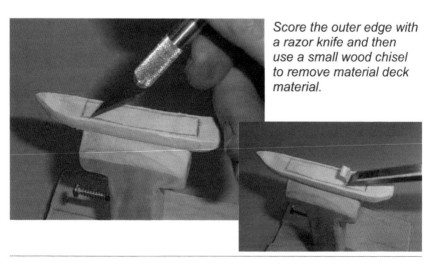

Score the outer edge with a razor knife and then use a small wood chisel to remove material deck material.

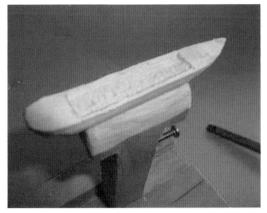

This area will have to be sanded flat but the effect of a deck with raised gunnels is well worth the extra time. Once the hull is sanded it can be stained or painted.

the entire hull by hand others use a pin saw or band saw to make the rough cuts and a dremel sander to finish up the rough design. The decks of the vessel can be recessed by scoring the outer edge with a razor knife and then using a small wood chisel to remove material. This area will have to be sanded flat but the effect of a deck with raised gunnels is well worth the extra time. Once the hull is sanded it can be stained or painted.

If you are going to paint I would recommend oil based paint. You can also use line tape available at most art supplies stores. The tape makes a nice straight line between bottom paint and hull color. Some additional details like hand rails, or ship's anchors can be added at this time.

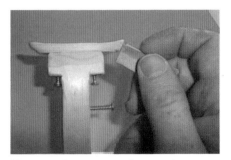

Fine sand paper can be used to prep hull and deck for paint or stain.

Use a pin vise to drill wire holes for hand railing uprights.

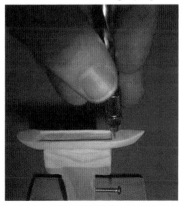

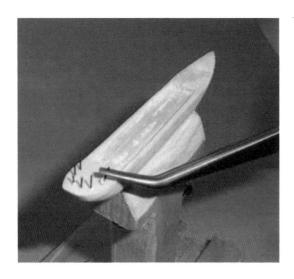

For handrails just drill snug, wire diameter holes around the perimeter of the hull's stern. Cut an adequate number of wire uprights. With a good pair of tweezers pick up one wire at a time and dip one end into Elmer's glue before inserting it into the drilled hole. Be sure to leave an empty hole at both ends. Once all of the hand railing uprights are inserted and the glue is dry you can trim them with a wire snip so that they are all the same length.

Once all of the hand railing uprights are inserted and the glue is dry you can trim them with a wire snip so that they are all the same length.

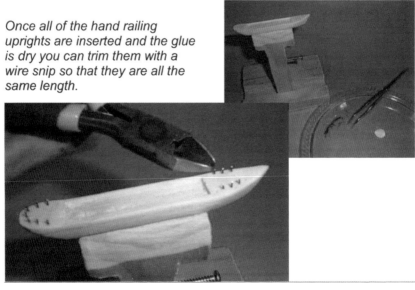

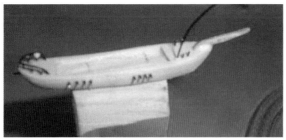

The top of the handrail is made from a longer piece of the same wire.

Wire just like hand railing uprights are inserted into side of gunnel. Standing rigging to support masts are wrapped around these wires. Once thread is in place a drop of glue is added to each to hold the thread in place.

The top of the handrail is made from a longer piece of the same wire. Dip one end into glue and insert it to the empty drilled hole and then carefully bend and mold the wire so it sits on top of each upright. Once finished be sure to glue each upright to the top piece. A small straight pin works well for applying just the right amount of glue to these small wires.

Bowsprit

The ship's bowsprit can be made using the same techniques as a mast. The shipboard end should be flattened on the bottom and can be glued in place to the hull with elmers glue. Additional detail can be added with the addition of a shorter support sprit glued under the original and wrapped with thread. It's very important for the bowsprit to be secure because it will be used to support all of the ships rigging and used to hold the vessels while it's being inserted into the bottle. Through out the project you should check the ships dimensions against your sketch and check the size against your bottle.

The shipboard end should be flattened on the bottom and be glued in place to the hull with Elmer's glue.

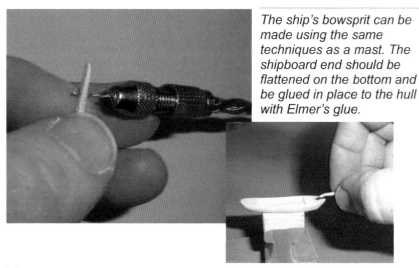

The ship's bowsprit can be made using the same techniques as a mast. The shipboard end should be flattened on the bottom and be glued in place to the hull with Elmer's glue.

Masts

Masts can be constructed from wood dowels available in most model shops. If the shop does not have round dowels you can use square stock. Square stock is actually sometimes easier to work with and drill holes into. Once the length is cut and all holes are drilled just use a little sandpaper to round the corners. The

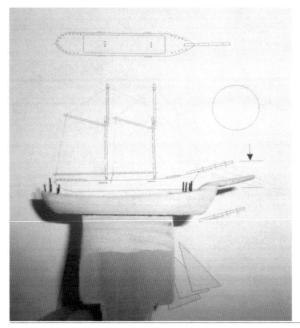

Throughout the project you should check the ship's dimensions against your sketch and check the size against your bottle.

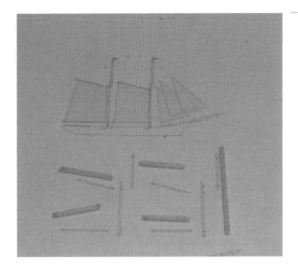

The most important factor in crafting masts is to refer to your master sketch. Each mast should duplicate the exact dimensions of the sketch and should have pre-drilled holes in appropriate locations for hinge, cross beams, and rigging.

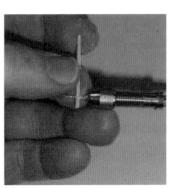

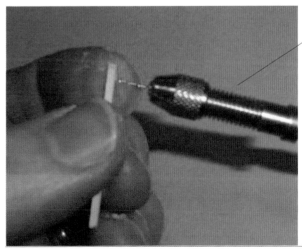

Pin Vise

alternative is to hand carve each mast. This is actually easier than it sounds. I usually just split a piece of wood off a block. I then use a razor to carve it into rough dimensions and then round the edges with sandpaper. The most important factor in crafting masts is to refer to your master sketch. Each mast should duplicate the exact dimensions of the sketch and should have pre-drilled holes in appropriate locations for hinge, cross beams, and rigging. It is

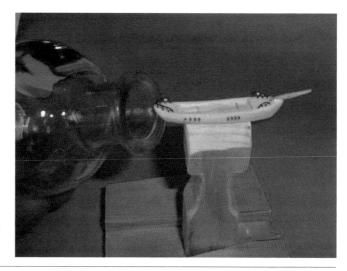

Confirm that your model fits into the bottle at each stage of the build.

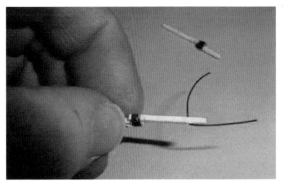

The hinge is a very simple, easy to make design. Insert a straight length of wire through a pre-drilled hinge hole. It should be a snug fit so your mast does not flop around. Then bend the wire on either side of the mast so it creates an inverted U shape. The two ends should extend at least 1/8" longer than the mast.

very easy to drill these holes before the mast is attached to the hull but a bit more difficult after. Please note that you will need to drill two different size holes in each mast. A smaller hole for wire hinges and a larger hole for thread. Diameter of drilled holes will differ based on diameter of wire and thread used. Basically the wire should be a press snug fit and the thread should be a loose fit. Please refer to illustration for details. Once the masts are completed and pre-drilled it's time to make the hinge and attach the mast to the vessel's hull. The hinge is a very simple, easy to make design. Insert a straight length of wire through a pre-drilled hinge hole. It should be a snug fit so your mast does not flop around. Then bend the wire on either side of the mast so it creates an inverted U shape. The two ends should extend at least 1/8" longer than the mast. Hold the mast in position on the hull and mark where each of these wire ends hit. Drill snug holes in the hull's deck and insert mast hinge ends into each hole. Your mast should now stand upright and be able to fold back toward the back

If you are going to paint I would recommend oil based paint. You can also use line tape available at most art supplies stores. The tape makes a nice straight line between bottom paint and hull color. Some additional details like hand rails, or ship's anchors can also be added at this time.

Ship and photo by the author.

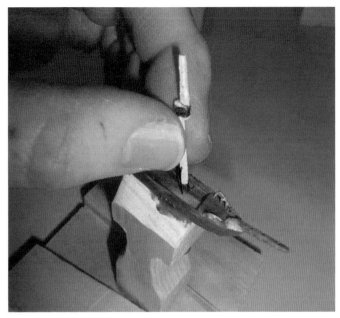

Insert mast hinge wire into pre- drilled holes in deck.

of the ship. One of the mistakes made during this process is not making the mast hinge hole high enough. This hole has to be as high as the tallest section on stern of model. Otherwise, rigging would prevent the mast from folding back. Repeat the same process for additional masts.

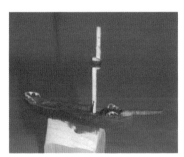

Image Left: Forward mast in standing position.

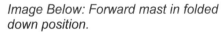

Image Below: Forward mast in folded down position.

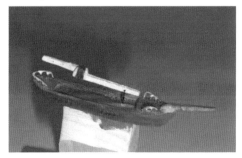

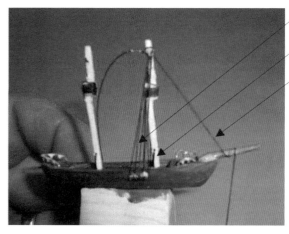

Mast supports

Mast hinges

Temp line holding mast upright while rat line glue drys.

Mast supports (rat lines)

Each mast must be supported with thread that runs from the upper portion of the mast down to the gunnels. Please refer to Basic Principles Illustration for details. I use a single length of thread for each side. Start by drilling 4, 6 or 8 (depending on size of your model) sung holes for wire along the side of the hull. Be sure to keep the forward

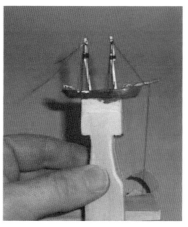

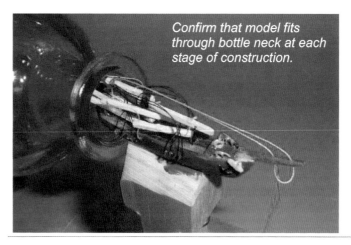

Confirm that model fits through bottle neck at each stage of construction.

Spars are held in place by twisting thread with glue letting it dry and inserting it through holes in mast. The extra string can be trimmed after glue dries.

Forward most wire must be even with the mast. If your wires are forward of the mast the thread would not allow the mast to fold.

most hole even with the mast. If your holes are forward of the mast, the thread would not allow mast to fold. Insert and glue a small piece of wire into each hole. You can also insert and glue a piece of wire into the pre-drilled hole on the top of each mast. Bend both ends of this wire upward so the thread will be less likely to fall off as you warp it into place. Now start at the top. Tie the thread onto the mast wire then bring it down and loop it around all of the hull wires. Now go back up and around the mast wire again and back down. This time only wrap the inner wires, repeat this process for the total number of hull wires. The thread can tied to the mast wire and then a drop of glue can be applied to

Ship with all masts, spars, rat ines and rigging in place. On this simple schooner only two lines run through the bowsprit to be used to raise her masts once inserted into the bottle.

Image courtesy Allposters.com

each wire so that the thread will not slide off. As you are wrapping each thread make sure the mast is vertical and not tilted to the left of right. Once finished, confirm that the mast can still fold backward. Now repeat for each mast.

Cross members (spars)
Depending on the type of ship you have chosen you will either have square or fore and aft rigged sails. In either case the sails and cross member supports must all pivot or fold along with the masts with the end result being the ship's sails being wrapped around the hull while being inserted through the bottles neck. For square rigged sails the cross member should have three pre-drilled holes. One in the middle for pivot attachment to the mast and one on either end for rigging. Please refer to illustrations. The cross member is attached to mast with thread. Insert a piece of thread through the middle hole and then back over the top. With a

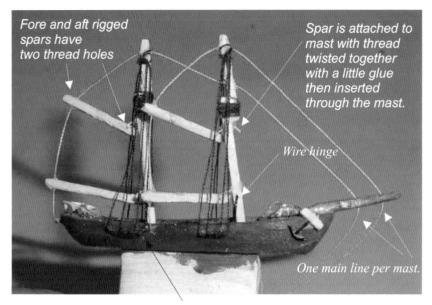

Fore and aft rigged spars have two thread holes

Spar is attached to mast with thread twisted together with a little glue then inserted through the mast.

Wire hinge

One main line per mast.

Standing rigging should be even or behind the mast. Otherwise it would prevent mast from folding back.

little glue twist both ends together. Once dry this creates a hard wire like pivot which can be inserted into position on the ships mast. Only put a small drop of glue on the back side of the mast. for fore and aft rigged vessels (as illustrated above) each spar needs only two drilled holes. One to attach it to the mast and one for the main line to run through.

Main Lines
Before even starting to rig your ship, note that a little Elmers Glue should be applied to the threads end and then twisted between your fingers. Once dry, use a razor blade to cut the thread. This leaves a very stiff sharp needle like thread which is much easier to work with and to push through all of your pre-drilled holes. Now start adding the main lines. Much like the mast supports start by drilling a snug wire hole in the stern directly behind her aft mast. Insert and glue a small length of wire. Start the rigging by tying and gluing a thread to this wire. The thread should be left long

The author uses a combination of epoxy casting resin, and silicone to create realistic waves.

enough to reach the outside of the bottle once the ship is mounted inside. Pass the same line through the pre-drilled holes in each mast and then down through the forward most pre-drilled hole in the ship's bowsprit. With each mast upright this string can be wrapped around the mounting bracket and temporarily held in place with masking tape. Do not glue this thread to any mast, spars or bowsprit at this time. Now repeat with the next line starting at the aft mast then running through the forward mast and then down through the second hole aft on her bowsprit. This thread can also be wrapped around the mount. Again, I use a small piece of masking tape to keep these threads in place. If your ship has three or four masts you will have to repeat the process for each mast. Basically, each model will have a main line for each mast. You will use these lines later to raise the ship's masts from outside the bottle.

The last step is to use white silicone to highlight the top of each wave. This creates very nice looking white caps.

Ocean in a bottle

While working on your ship model you can also prepare the sea scape which will add character and also be used to attach the model to the bottle. Most ship in a bottle builders use putty which is mixed with oil based paint. The putty is inserted into the bottle one tiny piece at a time, often with a handmade tool fashioned from a coat hanger. This method is very time consuming and the result does not always produce a realistic looking ocean. I prefer to use epoxy casting resin and silicone. The epoxy is used to form the base of the ocean. I mix the resin with blue paint until the desired color is achieved. I then use a funnel attached to a clear tube. The resin is poured through the funnel and into the bottle. This is a great method especially when working with large bottles. Do not attempt to remove the funnel tube until the resin is completely dry. I learned the hard way that smeared blue resin is very difficult to remove from the interior of a bottles neck! The next step is to mix some clear silicone with blue oil based paint and insert it into the bottle much like putty. Use a wire bent to form a small spoon to insert and craft the silicone into waves. Try

Epoxy casting resin mixed with blue oil paint can be poured into a bottle with the use of a funnel and tube. Be sure to let the resin dry completely before pulling the tube out.

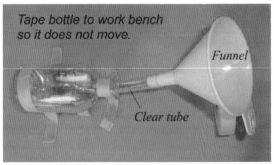

Tape bottle to work bench so it does not move.

Funnel

Clear tube

Wire coat hanger bent into a spoon and used to insert and form silicone into waves.

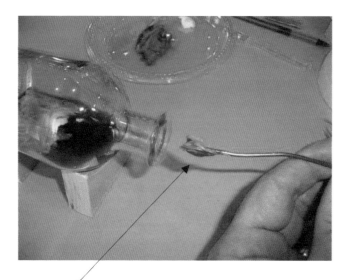

Clear silicone mixed with blue oil based paint can be inserted carefully into the bottle with a simple tool made from a coat hanger.

Mix of silicone and paint can be left with dark and light areas to help create a realistic ocean.

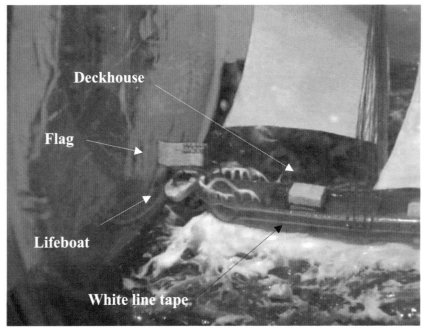

Deckhouse

Flag

Lifeboat

White line tape

Sea Scape is created with epoxy casting resin and silicone. Ship built by Capt. Dan Berg.

to create a pattern or realistic looking ocean. The last step is to use white silicone to highlight the top of each wave. This creates very nice looking white caps. White silicone will also be used as a base to glue your ship into place. Do not apply this until your ship is finished and ready to be inserted. Once your ship is all ready to be inserted through your bottle neck create a base of white silicone. The ship will be pressed into the silicone which should be slightly longer than the ship's length. Once dry, the silicone will securely hold your ship in place while creating the appearance of a ship's wash.

Additional details
Each ship should be as detailed as possible. Modelers can add lifeboats, deck houses, an anchor, a helm and even flags for detail. Most of these items can be easily fashioned from a small piece of wood, paper and some wire. Many of these details can be mounted to the ship prior to inserting it into the bottle. Others have to be fitted and then removed and placed on the ship after her sails are erected.

Ships anchors can be made from bending wire to form the bottom curve. A straight wire and wood spar will complete the detail.

Anchor

Ships anchors can be made from bending wire to form the bottom curve. A straight wire and wood spar will complete the detail. Once finished the anchor can be glued in place in the ship's bow.

Lifeboat

Lifeboats can be carved out of wood or can be crafted by cutting a small piece out of a toothpaste bottle. Once painted, either style can be mounted to your hull with two wires that form the life boat davits.

Deck house

A ship's deck house can be carved out of wood, painted and glued into position. Be sure to confirm that your mast hinges pivot high enough so the masts can still collapse sufficiently to get through the bottle neck even with the deck house in position. If not, you will have to install the detail after the ship is in position inside the bottle. To do this just use a little masking tape (like double sided tape) on the end of a wire tool. This will transport the house inside the bottle. Be sure to add a drop of glue. Then use an L shaped wire to hold deck house down and pull the house free from the tape.

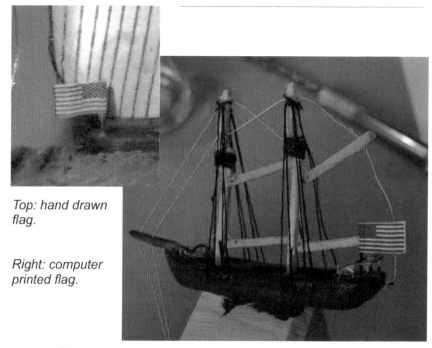

Top: hand drawn
flag.

Right: computer
printed flag.

Flag

Flags can be added to the top of each mast. These are cut from
colored paper and shaped and glued into position before the ship
is collapsed. A deck flag can be fashioned by drawing it on paper
and then cutting it out and gluing it to a straight piece of wire
which acts as the flag pole. Flag can be shaped around a pen to
make it look like it's blowing in the wind. I use a little artist spray
fix to hold flag in its desired shape.

*Deck Hatch cut from a piece of thin cardboard
painted black and glued to the ship's deck.*

*Coil of
rope
made with
tan
thread.*

Sails

Attaching the ship's sails is often the last detail prior to inserting the ship into the bottle. Sails are usually made from paper. You can dye the paper with a little coffee or tea for an aged look or you can buy a variety of art paper in different colors. Modelers can draw lines on the sails or leave them plain. Each sail should be cut from the original template and attached to its supports with glue. Each sail should also be shaped prior to gluing it in place. I usually use a little clear artist spray fixer which helps each paper sail hold its shape.

Inserting the ship into your bottle

Once the ship is complete, all paint is dry and additional details secure, it's time to get the tiny vessel into its glass container. Fold back all masts and wrap the ship's sails over the top of your ship's hull. Secure a set of tweezers to your ships bowsprit by wrapping masking tape securely around the tweezers. Now add a little white silicone to glue the ship onto your epoxy and silicone ocean. The

Computer paper stained with coffee and dried out completely. I have included a sail template sheet complete with fine lines. Just print it out, stain with coffee, dry and it's ready to be cut to size.

Be sure thread on forward sails does not get glued to sail but slides through folded paper.

Bottle with freshly added white silicone.

Detach your model from the work base and carefully fold mast and rigging back. The ship's sails can actually wrap over the model's hull.

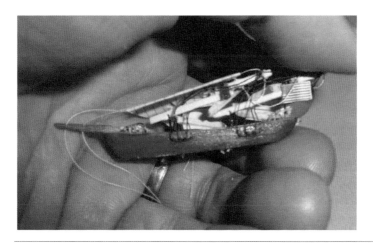

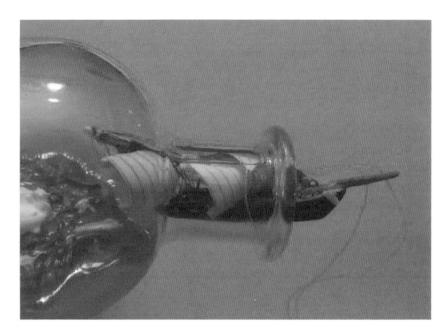

Now carefully insert the model through the bottle's neck. Be careful not to get any white silicone onto the model's sails or rigging. Once the ship is in place use an L wire tool to push the hull firmly down into the silicone.

Masts can be erected by pulling on the main lines and assisting with an L shaped wire tool. Once masts are upright and all rigging lines are taught use the same tool to place a small drop of glue to each bowsprit thread hole. Once this is dry, glue each mast and spar thread hole with the same tool.

After glue dries use a small razor taped to the end of a wire to trim the

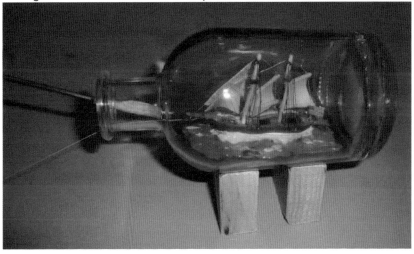

This tiny ship was crafted to fit in this apothecary bottle. Larger ships are actually easier to work on. Ship and photo by the author.

white silicone will end up looking like a ship's wake. Now, carefully insert your ship stern first into the bottle's neck. Holding the tweezers on one hand and an L shaped wire tool with the other, position the ship's wood hull directly over the wet silicone. You may have to slightly raise each mast my pulling on the strings that run from the ships bowsprit. Once you are sure no lines, or sails are low enough to touch the silicone, let the wood hull sit into the white silicone. Use the L-shaped tool to press the hull into the silicone to make sure model will be secure. Once the silicone is completely dry you can cut the tape to your tweezers and pull each mast completely upright. If needed the L-tool can be used to gently guide each mast upright. With the masts upright and rigging taught use a wire tool to glue each string hole on the bowsprit. Allow this glue to dry completely and then use a razor blade attached to a coat hanger wire to trim each string off the bottom of the bowsprit. Next position each spar and sail in place and use a tiny drop of glue on the tip of a wire to glue each pivot point and thread hole. Your ship is now basically finished. Just a few more details to complete the display.

Cork

After your ship is erected within the bottle it's time to finish off the display. Most bottles only require a cork to complete your maritime masterpiece. I would try to get a weathered looking cork or lightly burn a new cork to give it that aged look. If you used a screw top style bottle you might want to decorate the bottle neck to hide the threads. This can be done with a sailor's turks head knot. Any library will have a how to book with details on tying this fancy nautical knot.

Display

If your bottle is square or triangular it should sit flat on a display shelf and needs no additional mount. If you picked a round bottle you will need to build a mounting bracket to either shelf or wall mount the bottle. Check out some of the finished model images included in this book for display ideas. I especially like the idea of securing your bottle to a piece of driftwood. It makes a great display and adds a bit of nautical character.

QUEEN MARGARET
Four-Masted Barque

Ship in bottle model and photograph courtesy David Smith.

Check out more of David Smith's ship in a bottles
http://seafarer.netfirms.com

TITANIC *Passenger Liner*
This version of the Titanic was commissioned as a retirement presentation for the retiring head of the board of directors of a large corporation. His grandparents were scheduled to sail on board the original Titanic, but for some unknown reason changed their plans and never sailed.

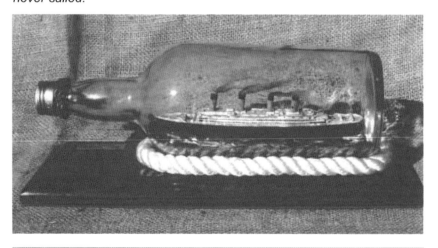

Three models of the Two-Masted Schooner **Bluenose.** The largest of these is 1 in 470 scale model shown above; the second, with a scale of 1 in 1500 is constructed inside a 50ml.

(2oz.) whiskey bottle and the smallest, at 1 in 1200 scale (.5" (10mm) long) is in an old cork-stoppered perfume sample bottle.

MARQUES Barque-Rigged Sail-Training Ship. Ship in bottle model and photograph courtesy David Smith. http://www.seafarer.netfirms.com

Franklin & Baltick. *American and British schooners that tangled during the US Revolutionary War. Ships in a bottle and photo courtesy Tom Netsel.*

Check out more of Tom Netsel's ship in a bottles
http://shipmaker.tripod.com/index.html

Puritan, *the winner of the America's Cup in 1885. Ship in a bottle and photo courtesy Tom Netsel.*

A Spanish galleon of the 15th-Century in a three-inch bottle. Ship in bottles by Tom Netsel.

Brigintine, square and fore-and-aft rigged sails helped these agile ships at sailing down wind or into the wind. Ship in bottle by Tom Netsel.

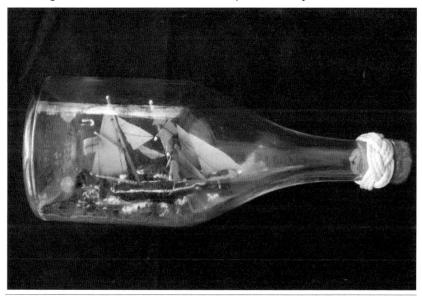

http://www.aquaexplorers.com/shipsinabottle.htm

Ship in bottle and photograph courtesy Artem Popov.

Check out more of Artem Popov's ship in bottles
http://www.shipbottle.ru/

*Kanoneer ship **"Koreets"** ship in bottle and photograph courtesy Artem Popov.*

http://www.aquaexplorers.com/shipsinabottle.htm

"Victory" Fernan Magallanes's ship.

Tasman's ship by Artem Popov

Galley "Dvina" by Artem Popov

Nautical Terms

Abaft: toward the stern of a ship.
Barque: a vessel of three, four or five masts. All are square rigged except the aftermast.
Barquentine: a vessel of three to six masts with only the foremast being square rigged.
Bowsprit: wood boom projecting from the bow to which foremast stays and jibs are attached.
Brig: a vessel of two masts which is square rigged on both masts
Brigantine: a vessel with two masts. The foremast is square rigged and the aft mast fore and aft rigged.
Gaffs: spars of a fore and aft sail.
Jib: staysail on a head stay.
Mainmast: the mast abaft the foremast.
Mizzen mast: the mast abaft the mainmast.
Ratlines: ropes across shrouds on which the crew climbed aloft.
Running rigging: rigging used to operate sails.
Standing rigging: Rigging which supports masts and yards.
Stays: ropes or wire that supports masts in a fore and aft direction.
Stay sails: triangular sail set on fore and aft stays.
Top mast: mast above the lower mast.
Yard: a spar that carries a square sail.

Image courtesy Allposters.com

Made in the USA
Lexington, KY
04 September 2015